Bones, Bones, Dinosaur Bones
by Byron Barton

Thomas Y. Crowell   New York

Bones, Bones, Dinosaur Bones. Copyright © 1990 by Byron Barton. Printed in the U.S.A. All rights reserved. 10 9 8 7 6 5 4 3 2 1. First Edition. Library of Congress Cataloging-in-Publication Data. Barton, Byron. Bones, bones, dinosaur bones / Byron Barton.   p.   cm. Summary: A cast of characters looks for, finds, and assembles some dinosaur bones.   ISBN 0-690-04825-4 : $. — ISBN 0-690-04827-0 (lib. bdg.) : $ (1. Dinosaurs—Fiction.) I. Title. PZ7.B2848Bo 1990 (E)—dc20 89-71306   CIP   AC

Bones. Bones. We look for bones.

Tyrannosaurus, Apatosaurus, Stegosaurus,
Ankylosaurus, Parasaurolophus, Gallimimus,
Thecodontosaurus, Triceratops.

We look for the bones of dinosaurs.

We find them.

We dig them up.

We wrap them

and pack them.

We load them on trucks.

We have the bones of dinosaurs.

We have head bones, foot bones, leg bones,

rib bones, back bones, teeth and claws.

We put the claws on the foot bones

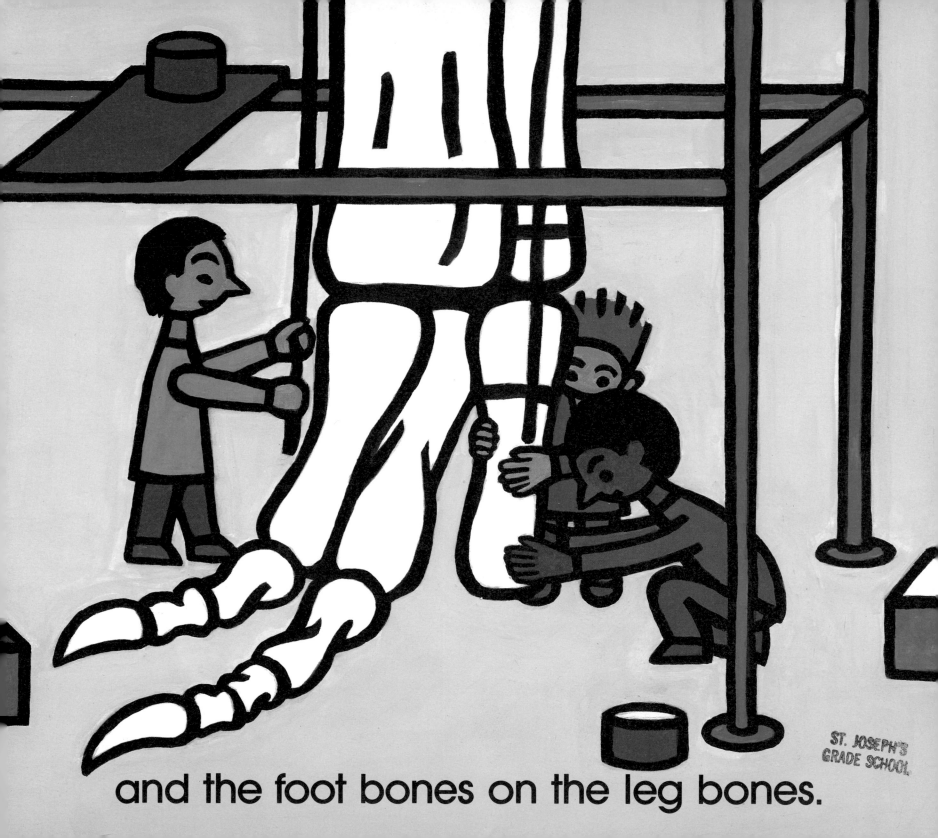

and the foot bones on the leg bones.

We put the teeth in the head bones

and the head bones on the neck bones.

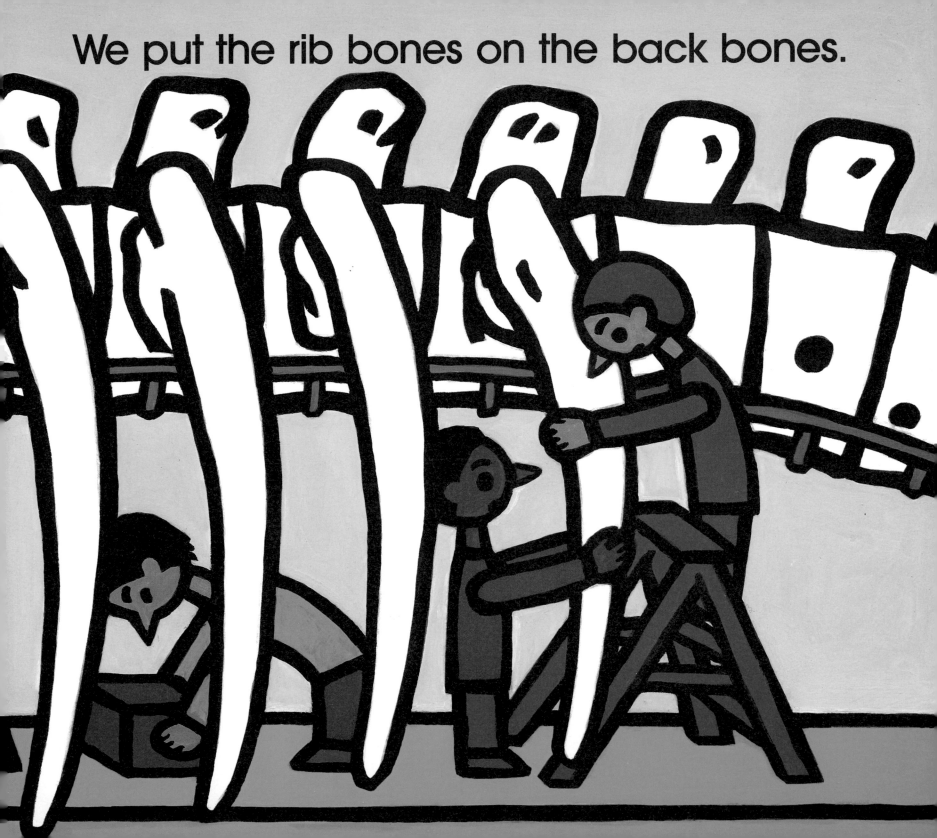

And the tail bones are last.

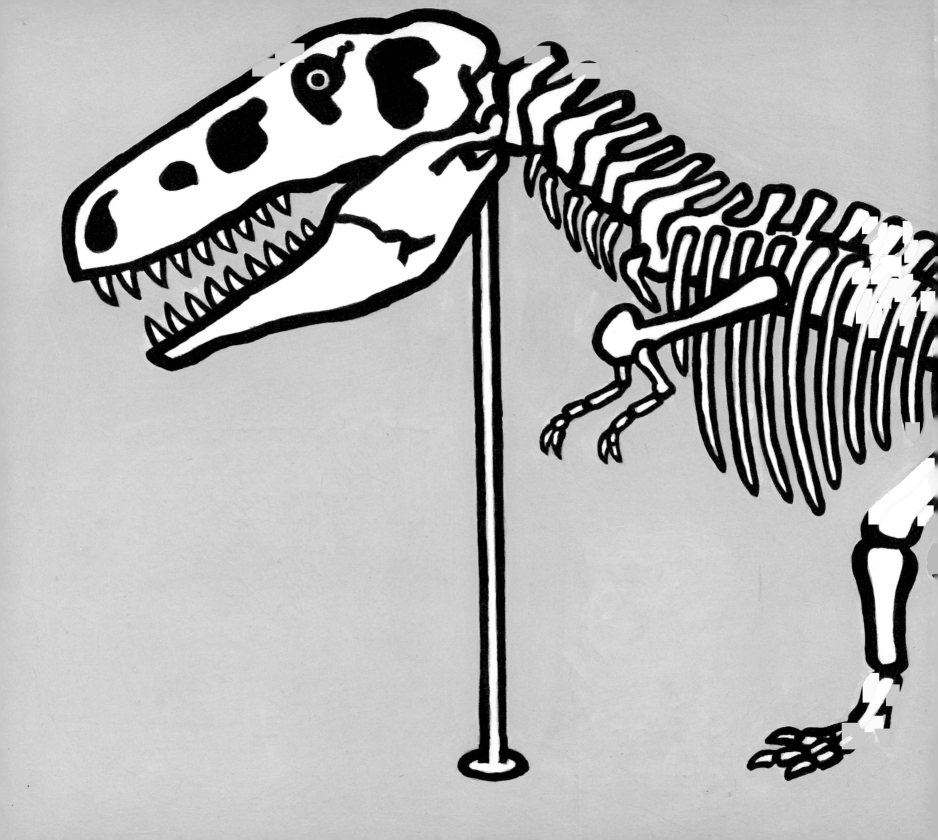

These are the bones of Tyrannosaurus rex.

Bones. Bones. We look for bones.

Apatosaurus
(ah-PAT-oh-SAW-rus)

Gallimimus
(gal-li-MY-mus)

STEGOSAURUS
(steg-oh-SAW-rus)

Parasaurolophus
(PARE-ah-saw-ROH-lah-fus)

Tyrannosaurus rex
(ty-ran-oh-SAW-rus rex)

Ankylosaurus
(an-KY-loh-SAW-rus)

Thicodontosaurus
(thee-coh-don-toh-SAW-rus)

Triceratops
(try-SARE-ah-TOPS)

We look for the bones of dinosaurs.